To:

_____

From:

_____

$\mathcal{W}$hatever you ask for in prayer,
believe that you have received it,
and it will be yours.

—MARK 11:24

Dear God: Wonderful Ways to Talk with Him
Copyright © 2000 by Zondervan

ISBN 0-310-98492-0
This edition published in 2001 by Zondervan
Publishing House exclusively for Hallmark Cards, Inc.

All Scripture quotations, unless otherwise noted, are
taken from the *Holy Bible: New International Version,*
(North American Edition). Copyright
© 1973, 1978, 1984, by International Bible Society.
Used by permission of Zondervan Publishing House. All
rights reserved.

The "NIV" and "New International Version" trademarks
are registered in the United States Patent and
Trademark Office by International Bible Society.

www.hallmark.com

Interior photos: Garry Black/Masterfile (www.master-
file.com); Comstock Images (www.comstock.com);
Corbis Images (www.corbis.com); Eyewire and Artville
(www.eyewire.com)

Printed in Singapore

01 02 03 /TP/ 6 5 4 3 2

Dear God

Wonderful Ways To Talk To Him

Hallmark
BOOKS

 Zondervan

BOK5041

Table of Contents

O God, let my moments
of prayer be quiet centers
in a noisy world—times when
I am conscious of your eternal
ways and know the strength
of your presence with me in
Jesus Christ. Amen.

—EUGENE H. PETERSON

Introduction

rayer covers the whole of a person's life. There is no thought, feeling, yearning, or desire, however low, trifling, or vulgar we may deem it, which if it affects our real interest or happiness, we may not lay before God and be sure of sympathy. His nature is such that our often coming does not tire him. The whole burden of the whole life of every person may be rolled on to God and not weary him, though it has wearied the person." (Henry Ward Beecher)

May this book lead you as you explore the many wonderful ways to talk with God, in your times of joy, in your times of sorrow, and whenever you need to know that you are not alone.

Everyday Prayers

You don't have to wait until
you are in a crisis or a difficult
situation to talk to God. Even
the little details of your life
are important to him.

Today, Lord, whether

I am at work or at home,

in the car or in my bed, may

your hand guide me and may

your light shine through me,

every minute of the day.

Amen.

*H*eavenly Father, you are the God who is intimately acquainted with my every need and desire. Thank you for concerning yourself with the details of my life.

—CHARLES STANLEY

Help me, O God,
To be a still axis in the wheel of activities that
    revolves around my life.
Deliver me from my distractions,
    which are many,
and lead me to a quiet place of devotion at
    your feet.

—KEN GIRE

*G*racious Holy Spirit, so much of my life seems to revolve around my interests and my welfare. I would like to live just one day in which everything I did benefited someone besides myself. Perhaps prayer for others is a starting point. Help me to do so without any need for praise or reward.

In Jesus' name. Amen.

—RICHARD J. FOSTER

*L*ord, I choose to be wise by obeying you. Nothing can compare to your blessings that come when I follow you. I know the danger of sin's consequences. Thank you for your grace to help me start anew each morning and for your Spirit to enable me to make the right choices.

—CHARLES STANLEY

*L*iving against the world's flow is difficult, Lord. I want your wisdom, but sometimes I seem to be caught up in so many of this culture's currents. I choose today to seek and pursue your ways. I make this decision in prayerful dependence on you to impart your wisdom to me and teach me your ways. I choose to listen to you daily so I may enjoy the benefits of godly wisdom.

—CHARLES STANLEY

*F*ather God, you know how easily I fall into bad habits in my thoughts, heart, and actions. Show me how to break one wrong habit and how to learn a godly one.

—JONI EARECKSON TADA

*T*ime is in your hands, Lord. Help me to remember that when the line in the grocery store is long, the phone won't stop ringing, or a friend indicates she needs to talk. Remind me to relax so I can be part of anything amazing you might want to do through me or for me.

—JONI EARECKSON TADA

Take to God your plans and failures,
   Anytime and anywhere.
No one ever goes unanswered,
For He answers every prayer.
He will answer every prayer,
He will answer every prayer,
Go to Him in faith believing,
He will answer every prayer.

—MARY BERNSTECHER

I will trust in you, Lord, with
all my heart, and not lean on
my own understanding. In all
my ways I will acknowledge you,
and you will make my paths
straight. (Proverbs 3:5–6)

—KENNETH BOA

Your mighty acts,

O God, have forged a path

of discipleship for me. Because

you go before me powerfully

and compassionately, I follow

in joy and in trust, through

Jesus Christ. Amen.

—EUGENE H. PETERSON

Prayers for Protection

In a world full of the
unexpected it is good to
know that there is a God
who watches over us all.

The eyes of the LORD are on the righteous
   and his ears are attentive to their cry. . . .
The righteous cry out, and the LORD hears
      them;
   he delivers them from all their troubles.
The LORD is close to the brokenhearted
   and saves those who are crushed in spirit.
A righteous man may have many troubles,
   but the LORD delivers him from them all.

—PSALM 34:15, 17–19

I need your protective help, Almighty God: be to me a refuge and a fortress. Grant that I may be more expectant of your protective care than fearful of the dangers of evil. For Jesus' sake. Amen.

—EUGENE H. PETERSON

༺

*L*et me walk in the ways of the upright and keep to the paths of the righteous. Let discretion protect me and understanding guard me. For the upright will live in the land and the blameless will remain in it.

—THE NIV WORSHIP BIBLE

༺

"Because he loves me," says the LORD,
    "I will rescue him;
    I will protect him, for he acknowledges
        my name.
He will call upon me, and I will answer him;
    I will be with him in trouble,
    I will deliver him and honor him.
With long life will I satisfy him
    and show him my salvation."

—PSALM 91:14–16

Do not be anxious about
anything, but in everything,
by prayer and petition, with
thanksgiving, present your
requests to God. And the peace
of God, which transcends all
understanding, will guard
your hearts and your minds
in Christ Jesus.

—PHILIPPIANS 4:6–7

*B*lessed are all your Saints, O God and King, who have traveled over the tempestuous seas of this mortal life, and have made the harbor of peace and felicity. Watch over us who are still in our dangerous voyage; and remember such as lie exposed to the rough storms of trouble and temptations. Frail is our vessel, and the ocean is wide; but as in your mercy you have set our course. So steer the vessel of our life toward the everlasting shore of peace, and bring us at length to the quiet haven of our heart's desire, where you, O our God, are blessed, and live and reign for ever and ever.

—SAINT AUGUSTINE (*modernized*)

O Lord, you are my hiding place;
you will protect me from trouble
and surround me with songs of
deliverance.
—PSALM 32:7

*F*ather, we thank you in Jesus' Name that there are so many of your servants around us to protect us. How wonderful it will be to see them in heaven, but what a blessing that they protect us now. Thank you for your continuing protection and love. Teach us by your Spirit to believe your Word about all the riches that are available to us. Teach us to accept them, and teach us how to use them. Thank you that those who are with us are stronger and greater in number than those who are against us. Thank you that you are with us, Lord Jesus, until the end of the world. Hallelujah, what a Savior! Amen.

—CORRIE TEN BOOM

If God is for us,
who can be against us?
—ROMANS 8:31

The Lord is faithful, and he will
strengthen and protect you.
—2 THESSALONIANS 3:3

༚

*L*ord, open my eyes to your past acts of salvation. Make me aware of your protective presence today. And give me faith, hope and courage to walk into the future, entrusting all things to your love and power.

—THE NIV WORSHIP BIBLE

༚

In you, O LORD, I have taken refuge;
let me never be put to shame.
Rescue me and deliver me in your
righteousness;
turn your ear to me and save me.
Be my rock of refuge,
to which I can always go;
give the command to save me,
for you are my rock and my fortress.
—PSALM 71:1–3

O Lord, when obedience to Your command leads me into the path of the storm and I find myself bailing water to save my life, give me courage to step out of the boat and walk with You on the raging seas. Help me not to fear or be distracted by my surroundings; rather, help me to keep my eyes of faith—the gaze of my soul—focused on You. Come to me when I am desperate, catch me when I fall, and bring me safely through the tempest to the other side of my troubles.

—THE NIV WORSHIP BIBLE

L ord, I want to know you better so that I may trust you more. You really are my refuge and stronghold. Teach me to run to you quickly so that I may find shelter in your everlasting arms. There I know I am safe.

—CHARLES STANLEY

This is what the LORD says—

"Fear not, for I have redeemed you;

I have summoned you by name;

you are mine.

When you pass through the waters,

I will be with you;

and when you pass through the rivers,

they will not sweep over you.

When you walk through the fire,

you will not be burned;

the flames will not set you ablaze."

—ISAIAH 43:1–2

Graces

Saying "grace" may seem
like an old-fashioned idea,
but a simple prayer can start your
day with refreshment, begin your
meals with joy and end your days
with peace. You can celebrate
special days or just everydays
by talking to God.

Our Father which art in heaven,

Hallowed be thy name.

Thy kingdom come.

Thy will be done

   in earth, as it is in heaven.

Give us this day our daily bread.

And forgive us our debts,

   as we forgive our debtors.

And lead us not into temptation,

but deliver us from evil:

For thine is the kingdom,

   and the power, and the glory,

   for ever. Amen.

—MATTHEW 6:9–13 KJV

In the Morning

O God, help us that we may rise up and follow you with joyful and willing hearts. Make us patient to do your will this day. Come to our waiting souls as swift as the light of the morning. Give us courage and hope to make this new day a day of victory. In our Savior's Name. Amen.

༄

O Lord, support us all the day long, until the shadows lengthen and the evening comes, and the busy world is hushed, and the fever of life is over, and our work is done. Then in your mercy grant us a safe lodging, and a holy rest, and peace at the last; through Jesus Christ our Lord.
—BOOK OF COMMON WORSHIP
(*modernized*)

I thank you, my heavenly Father, through Jesus Christ, your dear Son, that you have kept me this night from all harm and danger; and I pray that you would keep me this day also from sin and every evil, that all my doings and life may please you. For into your hands I commend myself, my body and soul, and all things. Amen.

—MARTIN LUTHER (*modernized*)

*O*ur Precious Lord, you have brought us safely through the night into this glorious new day. Waken our minds and stimulate our hesitating wills. Give us courage and patience in whatever trial may come to us. May we use to the glory of your Name the precious hours of today. The night comes soon. At the close of life's day may we receive your welcome into the Father's House: "Well done, good and faithful servant." In Jesus' Name we pray. Amen.

Lord, you have been our dwelling place
throughout all generations.
Before the mountains were born
or you brought forth the earth and the world,
from everlasting to everlasting you are God. . . .
Teach us to number our days aright,
that we may gain a heart of wisdom. . . .
Satisfy us in the morning with your
unfailing love,
that we may sing for joy and be glad all
our days. . . .
May the favor of the Lord our God rest upon us;
establish the work of our hands for us—
yes, establish the work of our hands.

—PSALM 90:1–2, 12, 14, 17

O most loving Savior, in the light of this new day may the sunshine of your presence shine upon our souls. Dispel the darkness from our minds and wills, teach us how we should walk and what we should do. We thank you for the opportunity of duties and responsibilities before us. Give us willing hearts that we may patiently and faithfully toil this blessed day so that, at its close, we can say truly, this was one more day's work for you. In your Name. Amen.

E ternal Father of my soul, let my first thought today be of you, let my first impulse be to worship you, let my first speech be your name, let my first action be to kneel before you in prayer.

—JOHN BAILLIE *(modernized)*

Because of the Lord's great love

we are not consumed,

for his compassions never fail.

They are new every morning;

great is your faithfulness.

—LAMENTATIONS 3:22–23

Mealtimes

Taking the five loaves and the

two fish and looking up to heaven,

Jesus gave thanks.

—MARK 6:41

❧

*B*ountiful Giver of every good and perfect gift! You are never weary of supplying our returning wants—grant, we pray, that the food of which we are about to partake, may contribute to the comfort and support of our bodies, and enable us to engage with more zeal in your service. We ask it for Jesus Christ's sake. Amen.

❧

*B*less our meal today, and may your Presence fill us with gratitude for all these abundant blessings. Amen.

*L*ord, will you never cease your kindly care over us, and may we also continue unceasingly to bless you for all your past and present blessings. In Jesus' Name. Amen.

❦

*W*e give you thanks for life and all its blessings. Give this food to nourish our bodies, and your Word of Truth to sustain our souls. Amen.

❦

*A*ll things come of you, O Lord, and for these and all your blessings we give hearty thanks, in the Name of Christ our Redeemer. Amen.

❦

The Lord satisfies the thirsty

and fills the hungry with good things.

—PSALM 107:9

*B*less, O Lord, this food to our use, and us in your service, through Jesus Christ our Lord. Amen.

O God, your mercies are fresh every day and call forth each day anew our voices of thanksgiving. Through Jesus Christ, Amen.

*O*ur Father, we ask you to bless the food before us to our physical needs, and feed our spirits with your truth, for Jesus' sake. Amen.

*A*lmighty God, we implore you to pardon our sins, to bless the refreshment now before us to our use, and us to your service, through Jesus Christ. Amen.

O Lord, we thank you for life

and the joy of living, for health

and strength, and for these

blessings fresh from your hand

of love. Through Jesus Christ,

our Lord. Amen.

In the Evening

Now I lay me down to sleep,
I pray the Lord my soul to keep,
If I should die before I wake,
I pray the Lord my soul to take.

O Lord, this glorious day has passed, and the evening time is here. May we invite you into our hearts as the disciples of old, "Abide with us, for it is evening and the day is far spent." Help us, O Lord, to relax after the perplexing problems of the day. Watch over us during the night and bring us to the new day with renewed spirit and blessed hope. In your Name, Amen.

I thank you, my heavenly Father, through Jesus Christ, your dear Son, that you have graciously kept me this day; and I pray that you would forgive me all my sins where I have done wrong, and graciously keep me this night. For into your hands I commend myself, my body and soul, and all things. Amen.

—MARTIN LUTHER *(modernized)*

Beyond the sunset's radiant glow
There is a brighter world, I know,
Where golden glories ever shine,
Beyond the thought of day's decline.

Beyond the sunset's radiant glow,
There is a brighter world, I know;
Beyond the sunset I may spend
Delightful days that never end.

Beyond the sunset's purple rim,
Beyond the twilight, deep and dim,
Where clouds and darkness never come,
My soul shall find its heav'nly home.

—JOSEPHINE POLLARD

Now, into the keeping of God I put
All doings of today.
All disappointments,
hindrances,
forgotten things,
negligences.
All gladness and beauty,
love,
delight,
achievement.
All that people have done for me,
All that I have done for them,
my work and my prayers.
And I commit all the people whom I love
to his shepherding,
to his healing and restoring,
to his calling and making;
Through Jesus Christ our Lord.

—MARGARET CROPPER

44

O Lord, we look to you for protection through the night. We know that you are able to keep us, for you will not slumber. You have promised to preserve us from evil: you will also preserve our souls. Help us therefore to commit our way to you, O Lord. We look to you to direct our paths. In your Name. Amen.

Jesus, tender Shepherd, hear me,
Bless Thy little child tonight.
Through the darkness,
    be Thou near me.
Keep me safe till morning light.

Special Occasions

Holidays and special
occasions are some of the
most wonderful times of joy
and renewal in our lives.
God rejoices with us on
these days and loves to hear
our prayers of thanks.

Thanksgiving

*O*ur Father, you have abundantly blessed this earth on which we live with great harvests. You have provided for mankind all things needful. May we ever rejoice in your great goodness to us. Help us to forget not all your benefits. This is a good land in which we live. On this day of Thanksgiving we thank you for our food, our schools, books and many churches. Above all we thank you for your Son, Jesus. May the words of the Psalmist be our prayer: "Bless the Lord, O my soul: and all that is within me, bless his holy name." Amen.

*H*elp me to make this holiday a memorable time for my family and friends. Thank you, Lord, for giving us so many blessings for which to thank you.

—JONI EARECKSON TADA

Christmas

*L*ord, I cannot comprehend that You, the Creator of the universe, took on flesh and were born of a peasant girl. You, the One who spoke galaxies into existence, became a speechless newborn baby. You, the One who gave the stars their light, veiled Your own glory and slipped unnoticed into the human race. You, the One who clothed all of nature in its boundless beauty and order, came to us wrapped in rags and lying in a feeding trough. The miracle of Your incarnation is all too unexpected, too mysterious, too holy for me to understand. I can only follow the shepherds to the manger and bow in astonishment and thanksgiving, glorifying and praising You for all that I have heard and seen.

—THE NIV WORSHIP BIBLE

*W*hat a Christmas gift you've given us, Jesus. You, the Lord of the heavens, have come down to save us. What glory!

—JONI EARECKSON TADA

To us a child is born,

to us a son is given,

and the government will be on his

shoulders.

And he will be called

Wonderful Counselor, Mighty God,

Everlasting Father, Prince of Peace.

—ISAIAH 9:6

O God, help us to remember that the dear Lord Jesus came to earth and dwelt among us. He is indeed Emmanuel, "God with us." Then if you be with us we need not fear, for you are more than all that can come against us. Fill our hearts with great confidence and hope. For the Redeemer's sake, Amen.

※

E mmanuel, God with us, words seem impossibly small and unwieldy to try to express the immensity of your love for me, and the gratitude I feel. Help me to live today in a way that would honor the sacrifices you have made for me.

—JONI EARECKSON TADA

Almighty God, we thank you for your only Son, Jesus, the only begotten of the Father, who took upon Himself our flesh, becoming one of us. Help us to live for you on earth, and may every day be as joyous as the day of Christmas. In Jesus' Name, Amen.

As each happy Christmas
Dawns on earth again,
Comes the holy Christ Child
To the hearts of men.
Enters with His blessing
Into every home,
Guides and guards our footsteps,
As we go and come.
All unknown, beside me,
He will ever stand,
And will safely lead me
With His own right hand.

—JOHANN WILHELM HEY

The New Year

Another year is dawning,
dear Father, let it be
In working or in waiting,
another year with Thee.
Another year of progress,
another year of praise,
Another year of proving
Your presence all the days.
Another year of mercies,
of faithfulness and grace,
Another year of gladness
in the shining of Your face;
Another year of leaning
upon Your loving breast;
Another year of trusting,
of quiet, happy rest.

—FRANCES RIDLEY HAVERGAL

Dear Lord of all my days,

   Help me this new year . . .

To show your love to all I meet,

To live in the joy of your presence each day,

To seek your peace and to bring peace to the
   lives of others,

To learn patience in every circumstance,

To remember the value of kindness and to show
   it whenever I can,

To grow in goodness and become more like Jesus,

To show faithfulness to you, my family and
   friends,

To demonstrate gentleness in all my relation-
   ships,

To have self-control so that your light will shine
   through me.

Amen.

—MOLLY DETWEILER

Jesus Christ is the same

yesterday and

today and forever.

—HEBREWS 13:8

Easter

Heavenly Father, thank you for sacrificing what was most precious to you in order to make it possible for me to know you. Give me eyes to see past the temporal and into the eternal. Remind me to measure every supposed sacrifice by the standard you set at Calvary and by the certainty of eternity. You have shown the way. I pray for wisdom and courage to follow.

—CHARLES STANLEY

Said the angel, "He is risen!"
Tell it out with joyful voice:
He has burst His three days' prison;
Let the whole wide earth rejoice:
Death is conquered, we are free,
Christ has won the victory.

—CECIL FRANCES HUMPHREYS ALEXANDER

The women who had come with Jesus from Galilee followed Joseph and saw the tomb and how his body was laid in it. Then they went home and prepared spices and perfumes. But they rested on the Sabbath in obedience to the commandment.

On the first day of the week, very early in the morning, the women took the spices they had prepared and went to the tomb. They found the stone rolled away from the tomb, but when they entered, they did not find the body of the Lord Jesus. While they were wondering about this, suddenly two men in clothes that gleamed like lightning stood beside them. In their fright the women bowed down with their faces to the ground, but the men said to them, "Why do you look for the living among the dead? He is not here; he has risen!"

—LUKE 23:55—24:6

O God, we thank you for the provision you have made for our salvation, even the giving of your Son, who suffered death on the Cross for us. We rejoice in the fact of the resurrection. Give us grace that we may follow in the Savior's footsteps, dying daily to sin, that we may live evermore with Him. In our Savior's Name, Amen.

⸈

Father, how liberating it is to know that my eternal security is in your hands, not mine. Once a saint, I am always a saint. Nothing can change that, and nothing can take away my home in heaven. It is Christ's work of forgiveness and indwelling life that makes my eternal security firm. Thank you for the remarkable peace this truth brings.

—CHARLES STANLEY

We welcome glad Easter when Jesus arose,
And won a great victory over His foes.
Then raise your glad voices, all Christians and sing,
Bring glad Easter tidings to Jesus, your King.
We tell how the women came early that day,
And there at the tomb found the stone rolled away.
Then raise your glad voices, all Christians and sing,
Bring glad Easter tidings to Jesus, your King.
We sing of the angel who said: "Do not fear!
Your Savior is risen, and He is not here."
Then raise your glad voices, all Christians and sing,
Bring glad Easter tidings to Jesus, your King.
We think of the promise which Jesus did give:
"That he who believes in Me also shall live!"
Then raise your glad voices, all Christians and sing,
Bring glad Easter tidings to Jesus, your King.

Birthday Blessings

O Lord, you have searched me
    and you know me.
You know when I sit and when I rise;
    you perceive my thoughts from afar.
You discern my going out and my lying
    down;
    you are familiar with all my ways.
Before a word is on my tongue
    you know it completely, O Lord.
You hem me in—behind and before;
    you have laid your hand upon me.
Such knowledge is too wonderful for me,
    too lofty for me to attain.
Where can I go from your Spirit?
    Where can I flee from your presence?
If I go up to the heavens, you are there;
    if I make my bed in the depths, you are
        there.
If I rise on the wings of the dawn,
    if I settle on the far side of the sea,
even there your hand will guide me,
    your right hand will hold me fast.
If I say, "Surely the darkness will hide me
    and the light become night around me,"

even the darkness will not be dark to you;
the night will shine like the day,
for darkness is as light to you.
For you created my inmost being;
you knit me together in my mother's womb.
I praise you because I am fearfully and
wonderfully made;
your works are wonderful,
I know that full well.
My frame was not hidden from you
when I was made in the secret place.
When I was woven together in the depths
of the earth,
your eyes saw my unformed body.
All the days ordained for me
were written in your book
before one of them came to be.
How precious to me are your thoughts,
O God!
How vast is the sum of them!
Were I to count them,
they would outnumber the grains of sand.
When I awake,
I am still with you. . . .
Search me, O God, and know my heart;
test me and know my anxious thoughts.
See if there is any offensive way in me,
and lead me in the way everlasting.

—PSALM 139:1–18, 23–24

Wedding Prayers

Most Gracious Savior, bless, we pray, these two who have just pledged themselves to each other in the bonds of Holy Matrimony. This, O Lord, is honorable, and signifies the union that exists between you and your Church. It was upon an occasion such as this which you did adorn and beautify with your own presence and first miracle in Cana of Galilee. We pray that the love of these two may be strong, holy and deathless. Grant that they may regard their home to be a sacred sanctuary, in which you, O Christ, shall find your place as the Head of the family. In your Name, Amen.

Jesus said, "At the beginning of creation God 'made them male and female.' 'For this reason a man will leave his father and mother and be united to his wife, and the two will become one flesh.' So they are no longer two, but one. Therefore what God has joined together, let man not separate."

—MARK 10:6–9

O perfect Love, all human thought transcending,

Lowly we kneel in prayer before Your throne,

That theirs may be the love which knows no
ending,

Whom You forevermore do join in one.

O perfect Life, be their full assurance,

Of tender charity and steadfast faith,

Of patient hope and quiet, brave endurance,

With childlike trust that fears no pain nor death.

Grant them the joy which brightens earthly
sorrow;

Grant them the peace which calms all earthly
strife,

And to life's day the glorious unknown morrow

That dawns upon eternal love and life.

—DOROTHY FRANCES BLOMFIELD GURNEY
(*modernized*)

Prayers for a New Baby

Our most Gracious God, we thank you for this dear one whom the Scriptures call "the heritage of the Lord." We pray that through teaching and example that this child will have fellowship with you. You have taught us that all who would gain salvation must humble themselves and become as "little children, for the kingdom of heaven belongs to such as these." May this little one be dedicated to you. O Christ, who took the children into your arms, take this child and protect him/her by your own love and grace. Grant, O Savior, that the parents may guide their home to walk in your way; and that every member of the family may have faith, obedience, and love. May they all join you one day in the heavenly family above. In Jesus Name, Amen.

*D*ear God, speak to my children in their hearts. Imprint your voice on their memories that they may learn to discern your voice from the voices of others. Amen.

❧

A prayer of blessing for you, dear child,
    May you always be aware of the beauty around you even in the seemingly mundane events of life. May you be blessed with family and teachers who allow you to express yourself and help guide you in your special talents. And may you grow into the knowledge that you are God's child, always surrounded by his love, his care, and his peace. Amen.

Graduation

I pray ... that the eyes of your heart may be enlightened in order that you may know the hope to which God has called you. ... I pray that out of his glorious riches he may strengthen you with power through his Spirit in your inner being, so that Christ may dwell in your hearts through faith. And I pray that you, being rooted and established in love, may have power, together with all the saints, to grasp how wide and long and high and deep is the love of Christ, and to know this love that surpasses knowledge—that you may be filled to the measure of all the fullness of God.

—EPHESIANS 1:18; 3:16–19

The LORD bless you
  and keep you;
the LORD make his face shine upon you
  and be gracious to you;
the LORD turn his face toward you
  and give you peace.
—NUMBERS 6:24–26

Dear God, You have taught us in your Word that we should fill our minds with whatever is true, noble, right, pure, lovely, admirable, excellent and praiseworthy. Reveal the truth of your word that "The fear of the Lord is the beginning of wisdom" to these young graduates. O Lord, open all our eyes that we may see the wonderful things you have in store for us in your Word. In Jesus' Name, Amen.

May the grace of the

Lord Jesus Christ,

and the love of God,

and the fellowship of the

Holy Spirit be with you.

—2 CORINTHIANS 13:14

Baptism

*L*ord Jesus, I thank you that even though you had no sin, you humbly submitted to the baptism of sinners. And to this simple yet profound act of obedience the Father responded with love and favor: "This is my Son, whom I love; with him I am well pleased." I thank you, Lord, that as I follow you into the waters of baptism I too will find the Father's love and favor. Please teach me to walk in the spirit of my baptism. Help me to live a lifestyle of repentance, in the delight of my heavenly Father.

—THE NIV WORSHIP BIBLE

A little Child the Savior came,
The Mighty God was His Name;
And angels worshiped as He lay
The seeming Infant of a day.
He Who, a little Child, began
The life divine to show to man,
Proclaims from heav'n the message free;
"Let little children come to Me."
We bring them, Lord, and with the sign
Of sprinkled water name them Thine;
Their souls with saving grace endow;
Baptize them with Your Spirit now.
O give Your angels charge, good Lord,
Them safely in Your way to guard;
Your blessing on their lives command,
And write their names upon Your hand.

—WILLIAM ROBERTSON

lmighty God, the help of all those in need, the life of those who believe and our hope for resurrection,

We call on you for this, your child, that by obeying you in baptism he/she will receive forgiveness for his/her sins. Receive your servant, O Lord, as you have promised through your one and only Son, who said, Ask and you shall receive; seek and you will find; knock and the door will be opened. So now give to us who ask; let us who seek, find; open the door to us who knock, that this, your child, may enjoy your everlasting peace and blessing and may one day come to live with Jesus in your kingdom forever. Amen.

—ADAPTED FROM
the Book of Common Prayer

"I know the plans I have for you," declares the LORD, "plans to prosper you and not to harm you, plans to give you hope and a future."

—JEREMIAH 29:11

Prayers of
Help and
Healing

God is the only one who can move the mountains that we all have in our lives from time to time. Mountains of heartache and despair, fear and sorrow, disappointment and hurt, the loss of loved ones and loneliness. The only way these mountains will ever be moved is through our faith. Not faith in faith, but faith in the living God, the one and only true God of the Bible. . . . Pray with faith. Put your faith to work—put it into action and see what happens.

—HOPE MACDONALD

In Difficult Times

Lord, I am caught off guard sometimes by unexpected problems. I find peace so elusive. I cannot get my mind off my problems. Help me to turn to you and know that you can quiet my storms with promises from your Word, with an assuring touch of your Spirit. I am so grateful you are with me in the storms.

—CHARLES STANLEY

Father, help me to sink my anchor deep in your promises. As life's waves broadside my boat, enable me to remember that every promise has its beginning and ending in Jesus.

—JONI EARECKSON TADA

I am grateful I can lean on you, Lord. There are days when I feel I cannot go on, but I know that you uphold me with your hand. Thank you that you never let me go.

—CHARLES STANLEY

Is any one of you in trouble? He should pray. Is anyone happy? Let him sing songs of praise. Is any one of you sick? He should call the elders of the church to pray over him and anoint him with oil in the name of the Lord. And the prayer offered in faith will make the sick person well; the Lord will raise him up. If he has sinned, he will be forgiven. Therefore confess your sins to each other and pray for each other so that you may be healed. The prayer of a righteous man is powerful and effective.

—JAMES 5:13–16

ᔕ

*F*ather God, enable me to bear up under my burden by your grace. Help me to remember that you have handpicked my circumstances to accomplish your purposes for my life. May I humbly submit to your choice for me.

—JONI EARECKSON TADA

*Cast all your anxiety on God
because cares for you.*
1 PETER 5:7

❧

I must confess, Lord, that there are seasons in my life that seem futile. When I don't understand, it is comforting and reassuring to know that you have a purpose for everything in my life.

—CHARLES STANLEY

❧

*H*eavenly Father, you are the God who knows my every care. You know the demands of this day. You are even aware of the added burdens tomorrow will bring. Remind me, Father, that you never intended for me to carry even one day's cares alone but that you have made yourself available to share and sometimes even bear my load. Remind me to pray rather than worry. Replace my anxiety with faith. Amen.

—CHARLES STANLEY

Come Lord Jesus, and abide in my heart. How grateful I am to realize that the answer to my prayer does not depend on me at all. As I quietly abide in you and let your life flow into me, what freedom it is to know that the Father does not see my threadbare patience or insufficient trust, rather only your patience, Lord, and your confidence that the Father has everything in hand. In your faith I thank you right now for a more glorious answer to my prayer than I can imagine. Amen.

—CATHERINE MARSHALL

Lord Jesus, help me to have faith through the crisis I'm in right now. Remind me of all the evidence you have provided that I might believe.

—JONI EARECKSON TADA

*S*tay with me, Lord, especially in times when I am disheartened. Show yourself to me, even if it is only for a moment. For your presence means more to me than my understanding. And seeing you when life doesn't make sense is better than not seeing you when it does.

—KEN GIRE

*L*ord, I place my fears in your able hands. Since you are in control of my life and love me dearly, I can trust you completely. Thank you for caring for me tenderly. I trust you to take care of my fears.

—CHARLES STANLEY

*H*elp me not to focus on the hammer and chisel of suffering, Lord, but on you, the Sculptor. Help me to yield to the chisel today. Change me. Reveal yourself in me. And be glorified!

—JONI EARECKSON TADA

*H*eavenly Father, thank you for allowing me to face what seem to be impossible obstacles. These obstacles serve as a constant reminder of my intense dependence on you. Thank you as well for the promise of your strength and sufficiency. It is a great comfort to know I do not face Goliath alone. Father, I am available. I am trusting you to make me able. Amen.

—CHARLES STANLEY

In Sickness

Heal me, O Lord, and I will be healed;
save me and I will be saved,
for you are the one I praise.
—JEREMIAH 17:14

❧

O God, you have such tender care over us, even as a mother comforts her children, you have promised to comfort us. Graciously regard those who suffer illness; visit them with your healing power. In your Name, Amen.

❧

O most merciful Father, grant to restore to health, we pray, your servant. May those who minister to this loved one be blessed in so doing. May all the means that are employed be used to the restoration of health to the body and mind. In Jesus' Name, Amen.

O Lord, in our distress we call upon you, for you have told us in your Holy Word to "call upon me in the day of trouble; I will deliver you." You have also said, "I will come and heal him." Have mercy on your servant who is ill. We thank you, our Father, for the skill of the doctors and nurses, and for the release you have prepared through the skill of your servants. O Lord, all of the skill and remedies are in vain without your blessing. Restore the strength of this dear one who is ill. Bring us all at last into your Heavenly Kingdom. Amen.

O God, by whose mercy we are surrounded in happy circumstances, help those who are poor and in need. While we have our joyous companionships and our friends and neighbors, let us not forget the fatherless, the friendless, the sick and the dying. Help them to realize that you are a friend to them and that you only have the power to bring them to a glorious life with you. Amen.

> *"For you who revere my name,*
> *the sun of righteousness will*
> *rise with healing in its wings,"*
> *says the LORD Almighty.*
> —MALACHI 4:2

Lord, teach me the art of patience while I am well, and give me the use of it when I am sick. In that day either lighten my burden or strengthen my back. Make me, who so often in my health have discovered my weakness presuming on my own strength, to be strong in my sickness when I solely rely on your assistance.

THOMAS FULLER
(*modernized*)

God of great mercy, we pray for those who are shut-in. Sustain them by the assurance of your presence. Lift them out of their despondency. May they have faith in you so that they may not become restless or discouraged. Give them the vision of the Cross-bearing Christ, who conquered pain and death. May the light of faith and hope radiate from their room, as your promise is claimed: "The eternal God is your refuge and underneath are the everlasting arms." Amen.

Lord, let your thoughts be full of pity and tender mercy to this poor sick child, for whose afflictions we are now concerned; and send him that relief and comfort from the load, or increase the strength to bear it; and deal gently and graciously with him, O Lord, beyond what we are worthy to ask at your hands, even for your own goodness' and mercy's sake. Amen.

In Grief

We give back, to you, O God, those whom you gave to us. You did not lose them when you gave them to us, and we do not lose them by their return to you. Your dear Son has taught us that life is eternal and love cannot die. So death is only a horizon, and a horizon is only the limit of our sight. Open our eyes to see more clearly, and draw us closer to you that we may know that we are nearer to our loved ones, who are with you. You have told us that you are preparing a place for us: prepare us also for that happy place, that where you are we may also be always, O dear Lord of life.

—WILLIAM PENN (*modernized*)

O Lord, you have made us very small, and we bring our years to an end like a tale that is told; help us to remember that beyond our brief day is the eternity of your love.

—REINHOLD NIEBUHR

*O*ur dear Lord, we now call upon you because death has invaded the lives and homes of these dear ones. Your Word tells us that "as one whom his mother comforts, so will I comfort you." Help them to know that you are very near to them, "closer than hands or feet" in their need. You, O Christ, have suffered so much that you have been called the "man of sorrows, and acquainted with grief." We claim your promise, "I will not leave you comfortless; I will come to you." Give these dear ones the assurance that they "sorrow not without hope." You are "the resurrection and the life." You alone have conquered death, and because you live we also shall live. In your Name, Amen.

O Holy Spirit of God, so many hurt today. Help me to stand with them in their suffering. I do not really know how to do this. My temptation is to offer some quick prayer and send them off rather than endure with them the desolation of suffering. Show me the pathway into their pain. In the name and for the sake of Jesus, Amen.

—RICHARD J. FOSTER

God will wipe every tear from

their eyes. There will be

no more death or mourning

or crying or pain.

—REVELATION 21:4

Giving Thanks

Count your blessings

Name them one by one;

Count your blessings,

See what God has done.

—J. OATMAN, JR.

For Loved Ones

Heavenly Father, with tremendous gratitude I thank you for mothers. Strengthen them, Lord, for the enormous responsibility placed upon their shoulders.

In Jesus' name, Amen.

—LUCI SWINDOLL

Lord of Truth . . .

You have brought people into my life who taught me your ways. People like pastors and professors, who graciously shared their hard-earned knowledge and modeled real piety. There were other teachers, too: my parents, friends, and members of my church family—the cookware salesman, the working moms and housewives, and the sheet metal worker—who taught me with their words and reinforced these words with their lives.

—FROM *Prayers from the Heart*

*L*ord, thank you for placing in my life people who taught me how to live. Help me to pass on the lessons.

—JONI EARECKSON TADA

ॐ

*L*ord God, you said, "It is not good for the man to be alone; I will make a helper suitable for him." And you, the Lord God, made a woman from the rib you had taken out of the man, and you brought her to the man. And the man said, "This is now bone of my bones and flesh of my flesh; she shall be called 'woman,' because she was taken out of man." For this reason a man shall leave his father and mother and shall cleave to his wife, and they shall become one flesh. (Genesis 2:18, 22–24)

—KENNETH BOA

ॐ

*T*hank you, Lord, for the joy of intimacy between a man and a woman in the covenant of marriage. It is a gift that we treasure. And we know, Lord, that this is but a shadow of the love that you have for your bride, your church.

—THE NIV WORSHIP BIBLE

A wife of noble character is her
husband's crown. . . .
She is worth far more than rubies.
Her husband has full confidence in her
and lacks nothing of value.
She brings him good, not harm,
all the days of her life.

—PROVERBS 12:4; 31:10–12

*S*everal weeks after we brought our baby daughter home, I remember thinking to myself, *This is incredible. I can't believe it. I'm a dad. I'll be a dad for the rest of my life!*

Our lives have been indescribably blessed with a little one (or more than one!) who has proven his or her ability to transform our adult sophistication and poise into a face-making, baby-talking embarrassment—a grown-up who tumbles on the living room floor or holds a tiny tea cup, pretending to lavish its delicious contents. It's laughable to realize what we've become. And we don't care what others might say. We are parents, and it's time to celebrate.

Today would be a good day to thank God for bringing such laughter into your life.

—ROBERT WOLGEMUTH

☞

Sons are a heritage from the LORD,
children a reward from him.
Like arrows in the hands of a warrior
are sons born in one's youth.
Blessed is the man
whose quiver is full of them.
—PSALM 127:3–5

Two are better than one,
  because they have a good return
    for their work:
If one falls down,
  his friend can help him up.
But pity the man who falls
  and has no one to help him up!
Also, if two lie down together, they will
    keep warm.
  But how can one keep warm alone?
Though one may be overpowered,
  two can defend themselves.
A cord of three strands is not quickly broken.
—ECCLESIASTES 4:9–12

∽

I thank you God in heaven, for friends. When morning wakes, when daytime ends, I have the consciousness of loving hands that touch my own, of tender glances and gentle tone, of thoughts that cheer and bless!

—MARGARET E. SANGSTER

For God's Provision

Thank you, O God, for giving me a splendid world in which to live and for living in that world with me; for providing this place for living and then entering the process of living itself; for being both Creator and Savior to me, in Jesus Christ, Amen.

—EUGENE H. PETERSON

Jesus, your gifts are wonderful. Help me to keep your gifts in perspective—I don't want them to have a deadening effect on my love for you. I want to preserve my wholehearted devotion to you, the Gift-giver.

—JONI EARECKSON TADA

Thank you, Lord Jesus, that your power is so great that I can do all things through you who give me strength. Amen.

—CORRIE TEN BOOM

*L*ord, sometimes you answer my prayers so quickly that my head spins. I am startled by your nearness and reminded of your goodness. Thank you for those astonishing times when your prompt answers to my prayers bolster my faith and revitalize my efforts to pray.

—THE NIV WORSHIP BIBLE

*T*hank you, Lord Jesus, that you have brought us to the ocean of God's love and that nothing can separate us from it. Thank you that your Holy Spirit allows us to see circumstances from your perspective so that we do not need to fear, even if the earth were to give way and the mountains were to move into the heart of the sea, as the psalmist says. Hallelujah! What a Savior! Amen.

—CORRIE TEN BOOM

*T*hank you, Lord, for your light of truth that makes my way both safe and pleasant. With the light of your presence you warm my heart. With the light of your wisdom you enlighten my mind. With the light of your Word you illuminate my path.

—THE NIV WORSHIP BIBLE

*L*ord Jesus, thank you for your sustaining power and everlasting arms that I can lean on.

—JONI EARECKSON TADA

ॐ

You care for the land and water it, O Lord;
*   you enrich it abundantly.*
The streams of God are filled with water to pro-
*   vide the people with grain,*
*   for so you have ordained it.*
You drench its furrows
*   and level its ridges;*
You soften it with shadows
*   and bless its crops.*
You crown the year with your bounty,
*   and your carts overflow with abundance.*

—PSALM 65:9-11

ॐ

I bless your great name, Almighty God. I look back over past years and remember the help I have known from your hand. Thank you for your strength shared with me, for your power exercised in me, for your being on my side. In Jesus Christ, Amen.

—EUGENE H. PETERSON

For Life

Every good and perfect gift is from above, coming down from the Father of the heavenly lights, who does not change like shifting shadows. He chose to give us birth through the word of truth, that we might be a kind of firstfruits of all he created.

—JAMES 1:17–18

*L*ord of all, I praise you for the beauty you spread out before me to enjoy any hour of the day or night. When I try to take it in, I realize it's too wonderful to fully comprehend, just as you are. I am grateful for all this.

—JONI EARECKSON TADA

Surely goodness and love will follow me
all the days of my life,
and I will dwell in the house of the
LORD forever.

—PSALM 23:6

I love you, Lord God. I adore you. I worship you. I bow down before you.

Thank you for your gifts of grace:

—the consistency of sunrise and sunset,

—the wonder of colors,

—the solace of voices I know.

I magnify you, Lord. Let me see your greatness—to the extent that I can receive it. Help me bow in your presence in endless wonder and ceaseless praise.

—RICHARD J. FOSTER

❧

Jesus said, "I have come
that they may have life, and
have it to the full."
—JOHN 10:10

❧

*L*ord, you've given me so much, when I think of all the things my body can do. I bless you for the gift of good health.

—JONI EARECKSON TADA

Many, O LORD my God,

are the wonders you have done.

The things you planned for us

no one can recount to you;

were I to speak and tell of them,

they would be too many to declare.

—PSALM 40:5

For God's Love

ord Jesus, We are contained within [the boundaries of your love]. We will never find the outermost limits of Your love for us. Your love is immeasurable, inexhaustible, inescapable, irrepressible, insatiable, irrational. O Lord, my deepest desire is to know Your love through personal experience and, in my limited capacity, to be filled from Your unlimited resources.

—THE NIV WORSHIP BIBLE

ou are One who says: "I am the LORD, your God, who takes hold of your right hand and says to you, Do not fear; I will help you." Thank you, Lord my God, for showing the wonder of your great love by saving me with your strong hand! (Psalm 17:7; Isaiah 41:13)

—THE NIV WORSHIP BIBLE

*J*esus, how sweet is the very thought of you! You fill my heart with joy. The sweetness of your love surpasses the sweetness of honey. Nothing sweeter than you can be described; no words can express the joy of your love. Only those who have tasted your love for themselves can comprehend it.

—BERNARD OF CLAIRVAUX

❧

*L*ord Jesus, I am moved deeply by the extravagant, excessive display of your love for me. I am gripped by the intensity of your desire and emotion for my soul. You take delight in me ... and my heart rises to take delight in you.

—JONI EARECKSON TADA

❧

*H*ow great is your love, O Father, that you have lavished on me, that I should be called your child—and I am! (1 John 3:1)

—KENNETH BOA

Could we with ink the ocean fill,

   and were the skies of parchment made,

Were every stalk on earth a quill,

   and every man a scribe by trade,

To write the love of God above,

   would drain the ocean dry.

Nor could the scroll contain the whole,

   though stretched from sky to sky.

—FREDERICK LEHMAN

We give you thanks that to all who receive you, Lord Jesus Christ, and believe in your name, you give the right to become children of God—children born not of natural descent, nor of human decision or a husband's will, but born of God. (John 1:12–13)

—KENNETH BOA

⌘

Lord, I'm grateful I'm not a what's-his-name in your eyes. I'm not a face in the crowd. You thought of me, formed me, and designed every unique, wonderful bone in my body long before the foundation of the earth. Touch my life today in the personal yet powerful way you have touched people through the ages.

—JONI EARECKSON TADA

⌘

Give thanks to the LORD,
for he is good.
His love endures forever.
—PSALM 136:1

⌘

Heavenly Father, I can hardly imagine what your unfailing, unceasing love really means. I do know that it is what I yearn for in my heart. Each day, grant me a more complete understanding of how much you really love me. Along the way, teach me how to express that love to those around me. Thank you for creating the need for love within me and supplying that need. Amen.

—CHARLES STANLEY

Prayers for Wisdom and Guidance

Every day we face a
myriad of decisions, some big,
some small. God is always ready
to help you make wise decisions
and to choose the right path . . .
all you have to do is ask.

In Finances

Oh Lord,

You look on me when I am working. You watch me when I am playing. You know when I am thoughtful, and you listen when I am praying.

Therefore, oh God, I take comfort in knowing that you are with me when I am staring at a huge pile of bills. Bills for food. Bills for the house. Bills for all the things my family needs to live healthy and productive lives. You have promised to provide all we need—if I will seek first your kingdom and its righteousness.

Amen.

—FROM *Prayers from the Heart*

I choose to pursue you, Lord, not wealth. Since you own it all, you will give me what I need as I depend on you. Let my finances be ordered by you and not by my impulses. I look forward to the freedom you will bring in this area as I obey you.

—CHARLES STANLEY

Do not store up for yourselves treasures on earth, where moth and rust destroy, and where thieves break in and steal. But store up for yourselves treasures in heaven, where moth and rust do not destroy, and where thieves do not break in and steal. For where your treasure is, there your heart will be also.

—MATTHEW 6:19–21

Father, you are the perfect picture of success. You keep all things perfectly balanced and in order. Give me the courage to turn my attention away from those things by which I tend to measure my success and to focus my eyes on you. Beginning today, I trust you to prosper me your way and according to your timetable.

—CHARLES STANLEY

$\mathcal{P}$recious Lord ...

I want to know you in a basic, informal way, without letting life's distractions hinder our relationship.

I want to pursue spiritual wealth rather than material possessions. I want to have plenty to keep me busy but not let my job define me. I want my best friend's smile to be worth more to me than any amount of money. In a word, I want to keep it simple. After all, true happiness is an internal state that I can cultivate for myself, not an external possession that I have to buy in a store.

Lord, I pray that you will help me stay focused on what truly matters. Help me look inside myself, inside my heart, for the things I most need in my life. Don't let me get caught up in the pursuit of worldy goods. And let me live my life so people will know I am both simple and rich in your Spirit.

Amen.

—FROM *Prayers from the Heart*

ord, I can picture myself holding on to so many things that are important to me. Give me the courage to open my arms, to release what I treasure, and then to enfold the blessings you bring in return.

—JONI EARECKSON TADA

The Lord Jesus himself said: "It is more blessed to give than to receive."

—ACTS 20:35

ou, Almighty God, are my source and my hope. From your gracious hand come life and blessings, wealth and honor. Indeed, "Everything comes from you, and we have given you only what comes from your hand." Teach me to be a channel of your provision—to not live in fear but in the joy of giving. . . . May I be found a trustworthy steward as I worship you with my giving.

—THE NIV WORSHIP BIBLE

Remember this: Whoever sows sparingly will also reap sparingly, and whoever sows generously will also reap generously. Each man should give what he has decided in his heart to give, not reluctantly or under compulsion, for God loves a cheerful giver.

—2 CORINTHIANS 9:6–7

In Relationships

Heavenly Father, sometimes I feel I have no special gifts to give. Help me to remember that it takes no extraordinary talent to say an encouraging word or to live a life of faith that encourages others. It just takes trust—and genuine interest in someone else.

—JONI EARECKSON TADA

Lord, direct me to a friend who will enable me to know you better, one whose walk will inspire me, reprove me, and build me into Christ-likeness. Thank you for the people you have already placed in my life and the ones you will direct me to in the future.

—CHARLES STANLEY

Do to others as you would have them do to you.
—LUKE 6:31

God, remind me how sensitively and precisely you have balanced your scales of justice. Keep me from rushing to conclusions about others. Enable me to turn any insights I do have into prayers.

—JONI EARECKSON TADA

I will do nothing out of selfish ambition or vain conceit, but in humility I will esteem others as more important than myself. I will look not only to my own interests, but also to the interests of others. (Philippians 2:3–4)

—KENNETH BOA

Heavenly Father, thank you for looking beyond my behavior and loving me anyway. Grant me the wisdom and the courage to do the same for others. As I encounter those whose company I don't particularly enjoy, remind me to look at the person behind the behavior. Amen.

—CHARLES STANLEY

I want to grasp how wide and long and high and deep is the love of Christ so I can love others in the same way. This is how the world will know that you are real, Father—by our love for each other!

—JONI EARECKSON TADA

I must admit, Lord, I have great trouble controlling my tongue. In fact, I can't. Unless you work in my heart to transform my thinking, my words will reveal the ugliness of sin. Cleanse me from my unrighteousness. Show me how to reduce my volume of words while you cleanse me and implant your wisdom in my heart. I want to bless others with my tongue, not hurt them. Make my mouth an instrument of righteousness through the power of the Holy Spirit, who resides at the [source] of my speech—my heart.

—CHARLES STANLEY

I can hardly understand your love, heavenly Father. You gave your only Son for my sins, and you continue to give me all that I need each day. Teach me to give of myself to others so that your storehouse of spiritual riches may overflow through me.

Lord, how I want your peace and love to fill my home. I understand that I must accept others and allow you to change them. Forgive me for any selfishness and show me practical ways that your love can flow through me to my family. Thank you.

—CHARLES STANLEY

O Lord God, who has given me the gift of sight, grant that I may see not only with the eyes of my head but with the eyes of the heart also, that I may perceive the beauty and meaning of all that I behold, and glorify you, the Creator of all, who are blessed forevermore.

—GEORGE APPLETON (*modernized*)

$\mathcal{T}$each me, Lord, to be more hospitable to visitors at my home and place of worship. Remind me that if I don't take the role of host, perhaps no one will. Help me to remember how I felt when I was a stranger but you welcomed me into the family.

—JONI EARECKSON TADA

$\mathcal{I}$ do not like confrontation, Lord; and when I do think about a need to confront, I usually get angry. Give me the courage I need to confront the problem your way, always remembering the undeserved love you shower on me despite my erratic behavior. I ask for your wisdom to help me know when to confront someone and when to remain silent. Thank you that your goal is peace and that I can count on your guidance.

—CHARLES STANLEY

For Spiritual Vision

I thank you, Father, for the voice of wisdom. It calls to us, it seeks us out and does not remain hidden. Its voice can be heard by anyone who will listen. Please give me ears to hear and a heart to understand, so that I may live by your truth, walk in your light, and grow in your grace and knowledge.

—THE NIV WORSHIP BIBLE

*D*ear God, let me see my life through the lens of your love, and so be able to discern in exact detail what you think of me and what you do for me in Jesus Christ. Amen.

—EUGENE H. PETERSON

Lord, keep us close to your heart, so that we see everything in and around us from your perspective. Then we will not fear because we know that you never make a mistake. Hallelujah! Amen.

—CORRIE TEN BOOM

Oh Father, we thank you that we are your children and that you are a good Shepherd. Teach us through your Spirit to hear your voice clearly. Thank you. Hallelujah! Amen.

—CORRIE TEN BOOM

Heavenly Father, thank you for providing me with a means by which I can be free. Thank you for paving the way through the death and resurrection of your Son. Now give me insight into your Word that I may uncover the liberating truths I so desperately need to make my freedom complete. And Father, don't let me get discouraged and quit before this journey is complete. Amen.

—CHARLES STANLEY

Thank you, Father, that you still speak to me today through your Word, my circumstances, and other people. I need to hear your voice. Teach me to be quiet and alert. I will wait on you and follow your counsel.

—CHARLES STANLEY

God of limitlessness, I confess that I'm often caught up in seeing the limits rather than the possibilities. Open my eyes, but more importantly open my heart, that I might see and believe.

—JONI EARECKSON TADA

When I see how great you are, Lord, my faith soars. You always answer my petitions and you are always working in me. Turn my gaze on you so that I can approach life with the boldness you provide. I am weak, but you are strong. I rest in your strength.

—CHARLES STANLEY

Help me, O God,

To treasure all the words in the Scriptures,

    but to treasure them only as they lead

        to you.

May the words be stepping-stones in

        finding you,

    and if I am to get lost at all in the search,

        may it not be down a theological

            rabbit trail,

            or in some briar patch of religious

                controversy.

If I am to get lost at all,

    grant that it be in your arms.

                —KEN GIRE

Prayers of Forgiveness

Humanity is never so beautiful

as when praying for forgiveness,

or else forgiving another.

—JEAN PAUL RICHTER

From God

*D*ear Father, ... Please forgive me for the infinite offenses to your goodness that I have committed today ... this hour. I'm not even aware of most of them. I live too unaware. That in itself is a sin against heaven. I'm sorry. Increase my awareness.

—RICHARD J. FOSTER

Who is a God like you,
   who pardons sin and forgives the
      transgression
   of the remnant of his inheritance?
You do not stay angry forever
   but delight to show mercy.
You will again have compassion on us;
   you will tread our sins underfoot
   and hurl all our iniquities into
      the depths of the sea.
   —MICAH 7:18–19

*L*ord Jesus, I am a sinner. I need redemption and forgiveness. I believe that you died on the cross for my sins. Will you forgive me and give me a clean heart and make me a child of God?... I want to be sure that I will go to heaven. I understand that you are calling me today to come to you. Lord, I come to you now and pray that you will forgive my sins, cleanse my heart, and prepare a place in the house with many mansions—the house of the Father. Thank you, Lord, that on the cross you accomplished everything to carry our—and also my—punishment; and that you have made me— yes, even me—a child of God. Hallelujah, what a Savior! Amen.

—CORRIE TEN BOOM

*T*hank you, Lord, that you want to pour out your love in our hearts through the Holy Spirit to each person who confesses his sin to you and is cleansed by your blood.

—CORRIE TEN BOOM

*H*eavenly Father, Forgive me for harboring anger toward you for the wrongs done to me by others. I choose to believe that you are intimately acquainted with every detail of my life, that nothing goes unnoticed. Thank you for the assurance I have through Christ. I am excited to see how you will demonstrate your faithfulness in the days and weeks ahead. Amen.

—CHARLES STANLEY

*O*nce I was a slave to sin. I sold myself out for nothing, but all the money in the world could not buy my freedom. So You bought me back with Your own life and set me free. Sin made me worthless, but to You I am priceless. I praise You, my Redeemer.

—THE NIV WORSHIP BIBLE

Forgive my hidden faults, O Lord.
Keep your servant also from willful sins;
    may they not rule over me.
Then will I be blameless,
    innocent of great transgression.

—PSALM 19:12–13

Everyone who calls on the name

of the Lord will be saved.

—ACTS 2:21

I worship You, Father, for Your great love and compassion, Your tender mercy, Your patience and kindness, Your restoration and forgiveness. You know our weaknesses and our propensity for sin. You see our helplessness, and You act on our behalf. As a father has compassion on his children, so You, our Father, have compassion on us. Your mercies never fail; Your love endures forever; You will never forsake us. You will always be true to Your name: Everlasting Father, Savior, Provider, Healer, Counselor, Prince of Peace, Mighty God, Friend.

—THE NIV WORSHIP BIBLE

*T*he birds have their nests and the foxes have their holes. But you were homeless, Lord Jesus, with nowhere to rest your head. And yet you were a hiding-place where the sinner could flee. Today you are such a hiding-place, and I flee to you. I hide myself under your wings, and your wings cover the multitude of my sins.

—SØREN KIERKEGAARD

*H*eavenly Father, you are the God who forgives. Thank you for forgiving me. Bring to
my mind those wrongs I continue to cling to. Give
me the strength and courage to forgive, as you
have so graciously forgiven me. Amen.

—CHARLES STANLEY

❧

*F*ather in heaven, help me to face the painful
events in my life, to acknowledge the hurt,
and to seek forgiveness from you. Thank you that
you readily forgive and heal.

—JONI EARECKSON TADA

❧

I acknowledged my sin to you, O God,
and did not cover up my iniquity.
I said, "I will confess
my transgressions to the LORD"—
and you forgave
the guilt of my sin.

—PSALM 32:5

The LORD is compassionate and gracious,
   slow to anger, abounding in love.
He will not always accuse,
   nor will he harbor his anger forever;
he does not treat us as our sins deserve
   or repay us according to our iniquities.
For as high as the heavens are above the
      earth,
   so great is his love for those who fear him;
as far as the east is from the west,
   so far has he removed our
      transgressions from us.
As a father has compassion on his
      children,
   so the LORD has compassion on those who
   fear him.

—PSALM 103:8–13

I praise You, Lord, for the incredible value You place on sinners! You do not passively wait for us to come to You. You actively, passionately seek us out of our wanderings and hiding places. Your pursuit is relentless. Nine out of ten is not good enough for You. Ninety-nine out of one hundred is still unacceptable. You are not willing that any should perish. You want all people to repent and be saved and to come to a knowledge of the truth. When You find us You carry us on Your shoulders into the safety of the fold. You rejoice over us with saints and angels. Thank You, Lord, for Your limitless, bountiful, passionate, merciful, fervent, unshakeable love!

—THE NIV WORSHIP BIBLE

For Others

Lord, will you show me if there is anything between you and me, between me and someone else, me and my parents, me and my children? Will you help me when I ask them for forgiveness and when I forgive them?

—CORRIE TEN BOOM

Heavenly Father, you have forgiven each one of us for so much. We have wronged you time and time again, and yet you continue to extend your grace to us. We must do the same for others, but often it is very difficult. Only through your Spirit can we begin to forgive those who have hurt us—either intentionally or unintentionally. Convict us, encourage us, and enable us, we pray. Amen.

—PHILIP YANCEY AND BRENDA QUINN

*L*oving Father, . . .

Help me to be an agent of change in my world, to make a commitment to dispel angry behavior and positively affect people around me. You have given me all I need to be happy, Lord. Teach me to smile and offer a helping hand instead of angry words. Guide me so my behavior reflects your love rather than my selfishness.

Loving Father, in your mercy, teach me that I can't control others, but I can initiate the healing process with what I say and do. Healing must start with me. Help me to be a shining light. Teach me how I can ease the anguish of those whose souls remain shrouded in darkness. Give me the grace to be better than I am, more forgiving, more loving, more caring. I receive it, Lord.

Amen.

—FROM *Prayers from the Heart*

"I waited patiently for the Lᴏʀᴅ; he turned to me and heard my cry." O Lord, vengeance is yours, and so is mercy. How many times you could have said to me, "I'll pay you back for this wrong!" Instead you showed me forgiveness. So who am I to demand revenge or vindication? O Lord, when I am mistreated please give me patience to wait for you—not for vengeance, but for deliverance. And I pray that you will give me the grace to forgive my enemies just as you forgave me when I was your enemy.

—THE NIV WORSHIP BIBLE

I choose to forgive those who have hurt me because you tell me that is what I am to do, Lord. How can I withhold your love from others when you so freely love me? Let me always take the initiative to extend your love to others.

—CHARLES STANLEY

∽

L ord, you fed and clothed me even though I was your enemy. You met my needs even though I did not say thank you. You spoke words of love to me even though I cursed you. And you died for me even though I sinned against you. These are the things you did for me. Now please fill me with your love for my enemies. Help me to see them through your eyes and to treat them with your mercy and kindness, so that they might also come to know your love for them in Christ Jesus.

—THE NIV WORSHIP BIBLE

*H*eavenly Father, you are the God whose forgiveness knows no boundaries. Just as you are constantly forgiving me, give me the wisdom to do the same for others. And in this way keep me free from the web of bitterness. Amen.

—CHARLES STANLEY

*L*ord, sometimes I forget how graciously you overlook my shortcomings and outright wrongdoings. Bring to my mind now anyone against whom I've harbored resentments. Teach me to extend grace to that person in your name.

—JONI EARECKSON TADA

As God's chosen people, holy and
dearly loved, clothe yourselves with
compassion, kindness, humility,
gentleness and patience. Bear with
each other and forgive whatever
grievances you may have against
one another. Forgive as the Lord
forgave you. And over all these virtues
put on love, which binds them all
together in perfect unity.

—COLOSSIANS 3:12–14

Praises

Our hearts soar when we

hear words like "I appreciate

you," "I love you," "You mean

a lot to me." Just as we find joy

in words of love and praise,

God delights in hearing our

praise, too.

You are great, Lord, and greatly
to be praised. Great is your power,
and of your wisdom there is no end.
And man, who is part of what you
have created, desires to praise you.
For you have stirred up his heart
so that he takes pleasure in praising
you. You have created us for
yourself, and our hearts are
restless until they rest in you.

—SAINT AUGUSTINE

Loving God

One thing I ask of the LORD,
this is what I seek:
that I may dwell in the house of the LORD
all the days of my life,
to gaze upon the beauty of the LORD
and to seek him in his temple.
—PSALM 27:4

Thank You, gracious Lord, for giving us the gift of free will. You do not force us to have fellowship with You; rather, You lovingly woo us into relationship. May my worship and praise come from a heart that is filled with thanksgiving to You. I willfully, joyfully, gratefully come to You, not to see what You can do for me, but simply to say thank You, I love You, and to spend time in Your presence.

—THE NIV WORSHIP BIBLE

Give thanks to the Lord, call on his name;
make known among the nations
what he has done.
Sing to him, sing praise to him;
tell of all his wonderful acts.
Glory in his holy name;
let the hearts of those who seek the
Lord rejoice.
Look to the Lord and his strength;
seek his face always.

—PSALM 105:1–4

*B*lessed be your name, O God. You never disappoint me; you hear every cry; you satisfy every need; you banish my fears. In Jesus Christ you are in all and have become all to me. Hallelujah! Amen.

—EUGENE H. PETERSON

God, our Father, we adore You! We,
Your children, bless Your Name!
Chosen in Christ before time, we are
"holy without blame."
We adore You! We adore You! Abba's
praises we proclaim!
We adore You! We adore You! Abba's
praises we proclaim!

—GEORGE WEST FRAZER
(*modernized*)

Finding Joy in His Creation

*L*ead us, O God, from the sight of the lovely things of the world to the thought of you their Creator; and grant that delighting in the beautiful things of your creation we may delight in you, the first author of beauty and the Sovereign Lord of all your works, blessed forevermore.

—GEORGE APPLETON (*modernized*)

*C*reator God, you've tucked so much beauty into each portion of creation that to try to take in even a little of it fills me with awe and wonder. Thank you that this is your world—no one else can own it. I'm grateful you've created it for us to enjoy. Teach me to pay more attention to the beauty with which you've surrounded me.

—JONI EARECKSON TADA

O LORD, our Lord,
how majestic is your name in all the
earth! . . .
When I consider your heavens,
the work of your fingers,
the moon and the stars,
which you have set in place,
what is man that you are mindful of him,
the son of man that you care for him?
You made him a little lower than the
heavenly beings
and crowned him with glory and
honor. . . .
O LORD, our Lord,
how majestic is your name in all the
earth!

—PSALM 8:1, 3–5, 9

My God and King, bird song and sea-roar accompany the praise I lift to you. Mine is no solitary voice raised in gratitude; a thunderous and multitudinous congregation is making sounds of thanksgiving, and I am glad to be a part of it. Amen.

—EUGENE H. PETERSON

Son of God, It is you who makes the sun bright and the ice sparkle; you who makes the rivers flow and the salmon leap. Your skilled hand makes the nut tree blossom, and the corn turn golden; your spirit composes the songs of the birds and the buzz of the bees.

Your creation is a million wondrous miracles, beautiful to behold. I ask of you just one more miracle: beautify my soul.

—CELTIC PRAYER

O God, I thank you
   for all the creatures you have made,
so perfect in their kind—
great animals like the elephant and the
   rhinoceros,
humorous animals like the camel and the
   monkey,
friendly ones like the dog and the cat,
working ones like the horse and the ox,
timid ones like the squirrel and the rabbit,
majestic ones like the lion and the tiger,
for birds with their songs.
O Lord, give us such love for your creation,
that love may cast out fear,
and all your creatures see in man
their priest and friend,
through Jesus Christ our Lord.

—GEORGE APPLETON
(modernized)

*I*t's yours, Lord—the earth and all that it contains. Remind me of my place in it. Not at the center of it all but simply as a part of your loving creation.

—JONI EARECKSON TADA

*G*reat and eternal God: I immerse myself in your creation. I am gradually beginning to comprehend the inventive attention you bring to each detail—and then I realize that I am one of the details! Hallelujah! Amen.

—EUGENE H. PETERSON

You are worthy, our Lord and God,
  to receive glory and honor and
      power,
for you created all things,
  and by your will they were created
      and have their being.

—REVELATION 4:11

The LORD wraps himself in light as with
  a garment;
  he stretches out the heavens like a tent
  and lays the beams of his upper
    chambers on their waters.
He makes the clouds his chariot
  and rides on the wings of the wind.
He makes winds his messengers,
  flames of fire his servants.
He set the earth on its foundations;
  it can never be moved.
You covered it with the deep as with a
  garment;
  the waters stood above the mountains.
But at your rebuke the waters fled,
  at the sound of your thunder they took
    to flight;
they flowed over the mountains,
  they went down into the valleys,
  to the place you assigned for them.
You set a boundary they cannot cross;
  never again will they cover the earth. . . .
How many are your works, O LORD!
  In wisdom you made them all;
  the earth is full of your creatures.
  —PSALM 104:2–9, 24

Praising God for Who He Is

You are holy, Lord, the only God,

    and your deeds are wonderful.

You are strong.

    You are great.

    You are the Most High,

    You are almighty.

    You, holy Father, are

    King of heaven and earth.

You are Three and One,

    Lord God, all good.

    You are Good, all Good, supreme Good,

    Lord God, living and true.

You are love,

    You are wisdom.

    You are humility,

    You are endurance.

    You are rest,

You are peace.

You are joy and gladness.

You are justice and moderation.

You are all our riches,

And you suffice for us.

You are beauty.

You are gentleness.

You are our protector,

You are our guardian and defender.

You are courage.

You are our haven and our hope.

You are our faith,

Our great consolation.

You are our eternal life,

Great and wonderful Lord,

God almighty,

Merciful Savior.

—SAINT FRANCIS OF ASSISI
(*modernized*)

Great is the LORD and most worthy of
     praise;
his greatness no one can fathom.
One generation will commend your works
     to another;
they will tell of your mighty acts.
They will speak of the glorious splendor
     of your majesty,
and I will meditate on your wonderful works.
They will tell of the power of your awesome
     works,
and I will proclaim your great deeds.
They will celebrate your abundant goodness
     and joyfully sing of your righteousness.
The LORD is gracious and compassionate,
     slow to anger and rich in love.
The LORD is good to all;
     he has compassion on all he has made.

—PSALM 145:3–9

Holy, holy, holy
*   is the Lord God Almighty,*
who was, and is, and is to come.
            —REVELATION 4:8

*O*God, you are my shield, my helper, my fortress, my deliverer, my strength, my refuge. You are my glorious sword, my eternal protection, my loving God. You are the horn of my salvation, the rock in whom I take refuge, the One who gives glory and lifts my head. My heart trusts in you and leaps for joy!

—THE NIV WORSHIP BIBLE

*I*praise you, Lord, for being so faithful, so consistent, so merciful and compassionate to me, even through—especially through—the hurt.

—JONI EARECKSON TADA

*G*od, I praise you for being all-sufficient. You have enough . . . you are enough!

—JONI EARECKSON TADA

*Y*ou are a God of great compassion and mercy. You love us with a love that is not rude, not self-seeking, not easily angered—a love that keeps no record of wrongs. This is the love of Christ. And it is to this kind of love that you call us, because it is with this kind of love that you love us. Lord, help me to love others the way you love me.

—THE NIV WORSHIP BIBLE

*H*eavenly Father, you are a God who rewards your faithful servants. You see and take note of all my labor. Thank you for the illustration of this that you have given us through your Son, who was greatly rewarded for his work on earth. Grant me the courage and endurance to keep on keeping on so that I may reap a reward at the proper time. Amen.

—CHARLES STANLEY

*Y*ou are a God who does not grow tired or weary, whose unlimited patience endures, whose compassions never fail. Great is your faithfulness!

—THE NIV WORSHIP BIBLE

*P*raise God! Your generosity expands each pleasure; your grace puts dimensions that are past understanding into every delight; joy crowns every gladness. All your words are beatitudes. Thank you, in Jesus' name. Amen.

—EUGENE H. PETERSON

*H*eavenly Father, you are the God who never sleeps or slumbers. You are the Master of all creation. You are the standard by which all things are measured. Remind me to approach all of life mindful of the fact that you are God. Amen.

—CHARLES STANLEY

Lord teach me to listen. The times are noisy and my ears are weary with the thousand raucous sounds which continuously assault them. Give me the spirit of the boy Samuel when he said to you, "Speak, for your servant is listening." Let me hear you speaking in my heart. Let me get used to the sound of your voice, that its tones may be familiar when the sounds of earth die away and the only sound will be the music of your speaking. Amen.

—A. W. TOZER (*modernized*)

Sources

Excerpts taken from:

Appleton, George, general editor. *The Oxford Book of Prayer*. © 1985 by George Appleton. (Oxford, London: Oxford University Press, 1988).

Boa, Kenneth. *Face to Face: Praying the Scriptures for Intimate Worship*. © 1997 by Kenneth Boa. (Grand Rapids, MI: ZondervanPublishingHouse, 1997). *Face to Face: Praying the Scriptures for Spiritual Growth*. © 1997 by Kenneth Boa. (Grand Rapids, MI: ZondervanPublishingHouse, 1997).

Foster, Richard J. *Prayer: Finding the Heart's True Home*. © 1992 by Richard J. Foster. (San Francisco: HarperSanFrancisco, 1992).

Gire, Ken. *Intense Moments With the Savior*. © 1994 by Ken Gire. (Grand Rapids, MI: Zondervan PublishingHouse, 1994). *Windows of the Soul*. © 1996 by Ken Gire, Jr. (Grand Rapids, MI: ZondervanPublishingHouse, 1996).

MacDonald, Hope. *Discovering How to Pray*. © 1976, 1990 by Hope MacDonald. (Grand Rapids, MI: ZondervanPublishingHouse, 1990).

Peterson, Eugene H. *Praying With the Psalms*. © 1993 by Eugene H. Peterson. (San Francisco: HarperSanFrancisco, 1993).

Prayers from the Heart. © 2000 by Honor Books. (Tulsa, OK: Honor Books, 2000).

Sanford, Don. *Prayers for Every Occasion*. © 1957 by Zondervan Publishing House. (Grand Rapids, MI: ZondervanPublishing House, 1957).

Stanley, Charles. *A Touch of His Freedom*. © 1991 by Charles Stanley. (Grand Rapids, MI: ZondervanPublishingHouse, 1991). *A Touch of His Love*. © 1994 by Charles Stanley. (Grand Rapids, MI: ZondervanPublishingHouse, 1994). *A Touch of His*

Peace. © 1993 by Charles Stanley. (Grand Rapids, MI: ZondervanPublishingHouse, 1993). *A Touch of His Wisdom.* © 1992 by Charles Stanley. (Grand Rapids, MI: ZondervanPublishingHouse, 1992).

Swindoll, Luci, Patsy Clairmont, Barbara Johnson, Marilyn Meberg, Sheila Walsh, and Thelma Wells. *Overjoyed!* ©1999 by Women of Faith. (Grand Rapids, MI: Zondervan PublishingHouse, 1999).

Tada, Joni Eareckson. *More Precious Than Silver.* © 1998 by Joni Eareckson Tada (Grand Rapids, MI: Zondervan PublishingHouse, 1998).

Ten Boom, Corrie. *Reflections of God's Glory.* © 1999 by Stichting Trans World Radio voor Nederland en België. (Grand Rapids, MI: ZondervanPublishingHouse, 1999).

The NIV Worship Bible. © 2000 by The Corinthian Group, Inc. (Grand Rapids, MI: Zondervan PublishingHouse, 2000).

Wolgemuth, Robert D. *The Devotional Bible for Dads, New International Version.* © 1999 by Robert D. Wolgemuth. (Grand Rapids, MI: Zondervan PublishingHouse, 1999).

Yancey, Philip. *What's So Amazing About Grace?* © 1997 by Philip D. Yancey (Grand Rapids, MI: ZondervanPublishingHouse, 1997).